Power for Daily Living

The Insight Series

Carl C. Fickenscher

CONCORDIA PUBLISHING HOUSE • SAINT LOUIS

Copyright © 1987, 2008 Concordia Publishing House
3558 S. Jefferson Ave., St. Louis, MO 63118-3968
1-800-325-3040 • www.cph.org

Written by Carl C. Fickenscher

Edited by Robert C. Baker

Scripture quotations are from The Holy Bible, English Standard Version®. Copyright © 2001 by Crossway Bibles, a publishing ministry of Good News Publishers, Wheaton, Illinois. Used by permission. All rights reserved.

Hymn texts are taken from *Lutheran Service Book*, copyright © 2006 Concordia Publishing House. All rights reserved.

Prayers are taken from *The Lord Will Answer: A Daily Prayer Catechism*, copyright © 2004 by Concordia Publishing House. All rights reserved.

This publication may be available in braille, in large print, or on cassette tape for the visually impaired. Please allow 8 to 12 weeks for delivery. Write to Lutheran Blind Mission, 7550 Watson Rd., St. Louis, MO 63119-4409; call toll-free 1-888-215-2455; or visit the Web site: www.blindmission.org.

Manufactured in the United States of America

1 2 3 4 5 6 7 8 9 10   17 16 15 14 13 12 11 10 09 08

Contents

About This Series 4

Participant Introduction 6

Session 1

    God at Work 7

Session 2

    Baptismal Exercises 16

Session 3

    Fruit Basket 26

Session 4

    Family Reunion.. 34

Hymnal Key

LSB = Lutheran Service Book
ELH = Evangelical Lutheran Hymnary
CW = Christian Worship
LW = Lutheran Worship
LBW = Lutheran Book of Worship
TLH = The Lutheran Hymnal

About This Series

This course is one of the Insight Series of short (four-session) adult Bible study courses, each looking at an important biblical topic or theme. Using these courses, you will gain insight into a portion of the Scriptures as you hear what God is saying to you there about Himself, about you, and about His Good News of salvation in Jesus Christ. These insights will help you as you go about your disciple's task of living in the Word and will equip you for a more fruitful study of the Word on your own in the future.

Using This Course

This course is designed to be used for small-group discussions. Each of the four sixty- to ninety-minute sessions you will find in this booklet will provide you with a clear picture of where the session is going and what it is supposed to accomplish, give you a way to lead into the session's study, provide input and discussion questions to guide your study of the text, suggest ways to follow up on the study during the week, and offer closing worship aids.

You will not need a teacher for this course. The printed material will guide you through the study. No one will have to be the answerer. But you will get the most from these materials if you:

1. Assign a leader for each session. That person should:

a. Make sure he or she works through the material before the session and, if possible, looks at some additional resources to enrich your study.

b. Begin and end the session with worship. The devotional time may be quite brief; a prayer or a Bible reading is sufficient. You might assign the opening and closing to a worship leader for each session.

c. Keep the discussion moving. There is a tendency to get bogged down on some questions. The leader should be willing to say, "We'd better move on to the next point."

4

d. Make some choices if time is limited. The leader will want to select those items from the session's content that seem to be most helpful if it is clear there will not be time to work through all of the material.

e. Listen. Make sure everyone is heard. Give each a chance to speak. Encourage participation.

f. Pray for all participants.

2. Prepare for each session. The discussion will work better, the material will be more meaningful, and the Word will speak more clearly if everyone in the class works through the session's material before the class session. Even if preparation is limited to reading through the texts that will be a part of the session's study, the effort will enrich your study.

3. Meet regularly (at least once a week) in a convenient and comfortable place. Too much time between sessions means that learning will be forgotten and much time will be used in constant review. Too little time between sessions does not allow time for you to connect what you have learned to your daily living.

4. Provide resources. Preparation that includes a chance to look at commentaries, Bible dictionaries, Bible reference books, maps, and so on will add to your class. Encourage those who do such research to contribute what they have learned or discovered as you study.

5. Encourage participation. The course offers many opportunities to discuss biblical texts and to talk about application of the Word to each individual's life. The key is sharing. Everyone should have a chance to listen and to be heard. The goal is encouragement. We want to build one another up as we study the Word. We want to share the hope and the strength we receive by the power of the Spirit through that Word. We want to allow each person to come closer to the Savior as he or she encounters Him in the Word. Emphasize the positive. Share the joy of the Gospel. Celebrate His promised presence as "two or three" gather in His name.

Participant Introduction

For many people Baptism is a singular, forgettable event that happened in infancy. God's Word sees it as something more dynamic. Baptism is our access into the family of God, but it is also our daily renewal in the forgiveness of Christ by the power of the Spirit. This study will allow you to look more closely at the meaning of Baptism in your daily living, help you to appreciate the resources God makes available to you through this Sacrament, and equip you to undertake a fuller commitment to living each day by the grace of God that comes through the Spirit at work in you.

os Session 1 so

God at Work

Our Goals for This Session

By the power of the Spirit working through God's Word, we want to

- rediscover the source and origin of the power of Baptism and its significance for our daily living.

Getting Started

Think of a situation when you were helpless, when you were not in control. Here's an example:

Paul and Cindy were driving along a deserted stretch of highway when their car began to cough and choke. It sputtered to a stop just as they came to an abandoned stretch of road about 15 miles from their house. Paul looked at his watch. It was 1:30 a.m. There were no phones, no houses. There were no cars passing by on the road. They opened the hood, and the mystifying complex halted any attempt to fix the car. They looked at each other in the dim moonlight and wondered, "What can we do?"

1. What about you? In writing on another sheet or in small groups describe your helpless situation.

2. What words did you use to describe your feelings in that situation?

Into the Word

While We Were Helpless

3. The amazing starting point of the Christian faith is this: we are helpless! Look at 1 Corinthians 12:3. Summarize what the passage says about God's part in our believing. What about our part?

4. See 2 Thessalonians 2:13. Compare this passage to the one above. Discuss the "actor" and the "receiver" according to the text. What does the text say about our part in believing?

5. In John 15:16, Jesus clearly indicates who chooses whom. Talk about what it means to be "chosen." What does that "choosing" say about our ability to "come to faith"?

The Spirit's Call

The Christian faith begins with the affirmation that we human beings cannot save ourselves. But there is more! The Christian recognizes the biblical truth that a person can't even believe on his or her own. It's not within his or her power to believe in Jesus Christ—or even come to Him. The Spirit of God calls a person to Himself. But how does He do that? Certainly not through a phone call or some kind of a mysterious summons to the throne of God. Here's the first major point at which Christianity differs from every false religion. It's God-centered, God-originated and God-initiated. Study Romans 10:14–17. Put the text into your own words. Then discuss the role of the Gospel ("Good News," "Message") in our believing. Why is it so important?

A Call for Sinners

Remarkably, God's love for us was "while we were still sinners" (Romans 5:8). It was for sinners—for helpless, separated-from-God people—that Jesus died. Perhaps that is also why Jesus used "birth language" to describe Baptism to one of the Pharisees called Nicodemus. Read John 3:1–5.

6. Nicodemus came to Jesus one night—a time when his religious friends wouldn't see him. Nicodemus was interested in what Jesus was doing. But Jesus had a surprise for this learned man who wanted to discuss religious philosophy with Him. Jesus said that if Nicodemus wanted to see the kingdom of God, he would have to be born again—actually, "born from above." What was Nicodemus's response to Jesus revelation? Why do you think he reacted as he did?

7. It was then that Jesus took the miracle of birth and elevated it to supernatural heights. He said that a person could not enter into God's kingdom unless he (or she) was born of water and the Spirit. What do you think Jesus was referring to? Why "water" and "the Spirit"?

8. Jesus compares Baptism to birth. Look over the passages above that talk about our part and God's part in our coming to faith. Why is birth a good comparison for the way God works in Baptism? Why can life after Baptism be called "new life"?

9. Some Christians talk about being "born again." We all were "born again" in Baptism. We were given new life by the power of the Spirit. What does that "birth" mean to you? How would you describe what happened to you in Baptism? How is the effect of your Baptism still with you?

For Forgiveness and Life

10. Read John 3:16–17. Summarize the truths of the verses.

a. Tell one another: Who is the actor? Why does He act? What is our reaction? What is the result?

b. Rephrase the verses in your own words. Why is this text called "the Gospel in a nutshell"? What does it have to do with Baptism?

11. With Baptism comes forgiveness of sins. Only God can give that gift. At the end of his sermon at Pentecost, Peter clearly links Baptism with forgiveness of sins. Read Acts 2:38–39.

a. Summarize the major points of these verses. What is Peter telling us?

b. Read Acts 2:41. What was the response of those who received Peter's message about Christ? How does that compare with our response?

c. How much did the Church grow that particular day? What does that growth say about the power of the Gospel?

Baptism Alive

12. Acts 2:42 tells about the growth that follows Baptism. List on the board the four activities of the Christian that are given in the text.

13. Birth is not an end in itself. People are born so they can grow up. Scripture says that Christians are to grow in both the grace and the knowledge of Jesus Christ (2 Peter 3:18). According to Matthew 28:19–20, what other important task should be part of a disciple's life?

14. In every church, there are members who are growing in Christ, and there are those who are caught in a rut of empty religiousness—just going through the motions of the Christian life. What are the implications of the birth of Baptism and the growth in Christ for your life? How are the activities listed above happening in your life? Write a brief description on a separate sheet, and share it with someone else.

Baptism as Renewal

As growing children of God, we are often caught in the temptation to rely upon ourselves. The story is told of the little boy and his father taking a walk on a cold, icy, wintery night. The boy insisted upon holding his father's hand. The father said, "Let me take your hand." "No," said the boy, "I want to take yours." But, as the boy reached up, he could only reach far enough to grasp one finger of his father's hand. As they walked along, the boy slipped and fell. His strength was not great. Besides, he was only hanging onto a part of his father's hand. The man picked up his son and grabbed his hand saying, "This time I will hold onto you." The boy reached out his hand, and the father put his big, strong hand around it.

That's what faith is all about. It's not reaching out and trying to grab hold of God. It is letting God take hold of you.

15. Think about, describe in writing, and then share with another person in your group a time you forgot how much God's power is needed. Focus on an event that reminded you how helpless you are. Discuss how that happening made you turn to the power of God in Jesus Christ.

16. Make a list. How does God show you that you are still like a baby in need of His care? Then make a second list. How does His power to forgive and renew you come to you? Through what people? How does the Word work in your life? Share your lists and insights with others.

Conclusion

Discuss the following summary statement. What insight is most important for you? Why? How can you use that insight to bring the Good News to others?

No one can make himself or herself a child of God. God does that. Jesus' death on the cross has made forgiveness available to all. That forgiveness becomes personal as the Spirit works faith in individual hearts—in Baptism by the power of the Spirit through the Word, people are born again of water and the Spirit. Baptism is not just an event. It's a way of life—a life filled with the power of God's grace.

In Closing

During your closing, ask volunteers to speak short prayers that bring some of the following to the throne of God:

- Thank God for your Baptism.
- Thank God for His forgiveness.
- Thank God for a new life from a new birth.
- Ask God to bless your ongoing Bible study about Baptism.
- Ask God to help you and your group members live your Baptism every day.

Some people look at Baptism as an event. Instead, it is the beginning of a new life with dependence on the Father, faith in the Savior, and power by the Spirit. In preparation for the rest of the sessions in this study, begin to think of ways you can remember your Baptism in your daily life. How can you continue to bring the blessings of Baptism and its assurance of God's continued love and forgiveness to mind? Make a list of practical suggestions that work for you. Bring your list to class with you next week.

Prayer: I yield You hearty thanks, most merciful Father, that it has pleased You to regenerate me with Your Holy Spirit, to receive me for Your own child by adoption, and to incorporate me into Your holy church. I most humbly beg You to grant, that I being dead unto sin, and living unto righteousness, and being buried with Christ in His death, may crucify the old man, and utterly abolish the whole body of sin. As I have been made partaker of the death of Your Son, may I also partake of His resurrection; through Christ Jesus our Lord. Amen. (Johann Gerhard, 1582–1637)

Close by singing or reading in unison "Baptized into Your Name Most Holy" (*LSB* 590; *ELH* 242; *CW* 294; *LW* 224; *LBW* 192; *TLH* 298).

Baptized into Your name most holy,
 O Father, Son, and Holy Ghost,
I claim a place, though weak and lowly,
 Among Your saints, Your chosen host.

Buried with Christ and dead to sin,
Your Spirit now shall live within.

My loving Father, here You take me
 To be henceforth Your child and heir.
My faithful Savior, here You make me
 The fruit of all Your sorrows share.
O Holy Spirit, comfort me
When threat'ning clouds around I see.

My faithful God, You fail me never;
 Your promise surely will endure.
O cast me not away forever
 If words and deeds become impure.
Have mercy when I come defiled;
Forgive, lift up, restore Your child.

All that I am and love most dearly—
 Receive it all, O Lord, from me.
Let me confess my faith sincerely;
 Help me Your faithful child to be!
Let nothing that I am or own
Serve any will but Yours alone.

☙ Session 2 ❧

Baptismal Exercises

Our Goals for This Session

By the power of the Spirit working through God's Word, we want to

- by the power of the Spirit through the Word be able to "exercise" Christian life in the context of our baptismal grace.

Getting Started

A man got all dressed up to go to a party. He was dressed in the fanciest clothes. Suddenly he fell over on the floor. A doctor nearby came running. After trying unsuccessfully to revive the man, she said, "It's too late—he's gone." Then she said to those who were standing around, "What religion was he?" And the people said he was an unbeliever. "That's too bad," said the doctor. "He's all dressed up with no place to go."

Read Galatians 3:26–27. In these verses, the apostle Paul speaks of Baptism as a garment. To "put on Christ" is to be clothed with Christ's righteousness. This is what happens when you receive the Holy Spirit in Baptism and believe in your Savior.

17. Look for a minute at the people in your group. Pick partners, and examine what each other is wearing. What do the outer garments tell you about the person? Jot down your observations, and discuss them with the group.

18. Read Galatians 3:26–27 again. What are some of the outward signs of one who has been baptized and has "put on Christ"? Talk about how those signs are evident in you and in those around you. In what sense is it true that Christians give evidence of their faith in their lives?

Into the Word

Your Personal Easter Experience

19. The Bible indicates that when you are baptized, you go through a personal Easter experience.

a. Read Romans 6:4. To what purpose are you "resurrected" in Baptism?

b. Read verse 5. How sure is the promise? How do you know?

c. Read verse 6. What has happened to you in Baptism?

d. What is the result in your life (vv. 7– 11)?

20. Many have popularized the saying "Today is the first day of the rest of your life." In Baptism that is really true. As a baptized Christian, you live in God's grace, His forgiveness. You live in relationship with your Savior and Lord, Jesus Christ. It's a baptismal lifestyle. What do the words of Galatians 2:20 mean specifically for you?

Exercising Baptism

Baptism can be compared to one of the body's muscles. By God's beautiful miracle of birth, we are born with many marvelous muscles that help us move and act. But as marvelous as muscles are, when they are not used, they atrophy. We have all seen muscles that have been inactive for a time. They wither from lack of exercise, shrink, and become almost useless.

An atrophied muscle is still there. It has only lost its power to act. For some, their use of Baptism is quite similar. Baptism is a gift with the potential for much good in a person's life. But sometimes our use of it becomes atrophied.

21. Unfortunately, there are people who have a baptismal certificate sitting in a drawer someplace who think little or nothing about their Baptism. What do you think leads to that kind of attitude? On a separate sheet or on the board, write

down some things you might do to help people make sure their Baptisms are exercised.

22. You may know many who have failed to exercise their Baptisms. Perhaps there was a time in your own life when the use of your Baptism was in a state of atrophy. Some people say that at that time we need to be rebaptized. But Baptism does not depend on our response to be effective. When Baptism slips into disuse, what do we need? Talk about how you were helped at such a time. How can we "get the Word out" to those whose use of Baptism has atrophied?

23. Exercise is an interesting phenomenon. Physicians say it's good to exercise, but you have to do it regularly. To be inactive for six months and then decide to strenuously exercise for eight hours in order to make up for the lost time is not only dangerous to your health, it doesn't work! Martin Luther had a nice way of saying Christians should exercise their Baptisms every day. He said that every day we should drown the old nature (old Adam). Each day we are to repent and turn away from our sins as we turn toward God and His promise of forgiveness in faith. Luther says that as the believer does that, he or she goes through a daily resurrection and comes forth a new person who intends to live—by God's help and with His power—in that right relationship to Him.

a. Talk about what that daily renewal means for you.

b. Share helpful ways you have found to remember your Baptism. Make a list of your own, and then compare it to others' lists.

24. Look at 2 Corinthians 5:17; 1 Corinthians 15:22; and Revelation 21:5. If a Christian feels badly about some recent sin, what is the real, joyful hope you find in these passages. Put that hope into your own words. Share it with someone else.

Baptismal Birthday

Exercising your Baptism might begin with remembering your baptismal (re)birthday. Almost everyone knows his or her physical birthday. In fact, celebrating birth dates is a great custom. It helps us remember that our lives are important. But what about your Baptism (re)birth date? Your Baptism was a historic event that marked the beginning of a new lifetime—an eternity with Jesus.

25. How many of the group know their baptismal (re)birth dates? How many celebrate them? How do they celebrate them? Talk about it.

26. Among many Christians, the world's birthday celebrations are part of life—but the Christian rebirth is hardly noticed. Read Romans 12:1–2. In what ways are we conformed

to the world? In what ways has Baptism called Christians to be transformed?

27. Make an action plan. Decide how you will celebrate Baptism (re)birth dates in your home, with your relatives and in your church. Write out your plan, and share it with others in your congregation.

Reminders

A once a year reminder is a great start. But it is hardly exercising your Baptism daily. What else can be done? The word *baptize* simply means to wash. In the New Testament, the original language says that the people washed (baptized) their dishes, pots, and pans (Mark 7:4). God took this everyday word and gave it powerful meaning.

28. Read Ephesians 5:25–27. What is the reference to Baptism? What are the implications for those who are baptized?

29. How can you use an everyday event like washing to remind you of your Baptism? For example, when you take a bath or a shower, you might be reminded that in the washing of Baptism your sins are washed away and your life is made clean. What other ways can you think of to remember your Baptism through your daily routines?

Power for Change

Notice the enormous potential for change due to the effects of Baptism and a new relationship with Jesus Christ! Read 1 Corinthians 6:9–11.

30. Look again at Ephesians 5:25–27. What is the connection between Baptism and the Word? Why is that connection important?

31. Discuss the close connection between baptizing and teaching (or learning from the Scriptures) in the act of making disciples (Matthew 28:18–20). Why is that connection important as we reach new people with the Gospel?

32. See Ephesians 6:4. What special responsibility do fathers have as they help their children grow up and exercise their Baptisms?

33. Discuss other ways the family can exercise Baptism. What do Bible reading, prayers, times of informal worship, and the like have to do with remembering Baptism? What other ways to remember the benefits of Baptism can you list?

Conclusion

Read the following summary statement and discuss it. What does it mean for you now? What does it mean for your daily living? Talk about your responses.

The means of grace are the channels through which God gives the free gift of forgiveness. These channels of His grace are the Word and the Sacraments. Baptism is one of these sacraments. It is a one-time act that begins a living relationship with Jesus Christ by the power of the Spirit. The other sacrament is Holy Communion, in which God repeatedly gives forgiveness through the body and blood of Christ that is shared with us as we attend His table. In Holy Communion, or the Lord's Supper, the forgiveness for which Jesus paid dearly on the cross becomes personal in the life of a Christian. Thank God for His Word and Sacraments.

In Closing

Ask volunteers to include some of the following in short prayers offered in the name of the whole class:

- Ask God to bless you as you exercise your Baptism.
- Ask God to touch the lives of those who do not exercise their Baptisms.
- Ask God to help you help others to live and daily celebrate the gift of forgiveness in Baptism.

Exercise takes discipline. The word *discipline* comes from the same root word as the word *disciple*. To exercise your Baptism takes some discipline. It involves living in daily repentance, looking to the Word, believing God's promises in Christ, praying to God diligently, renouncing the devil, and pledging allegiance to Jesus.

Read Job 42:1–2. Reflect on the promise you find there. What mechanisms of discipline do you or can you use for exercising your Baptism? Please list them. Plan to use them. At your next class session, share your experiences exercising your Baptism.

Prayer: Lord, my God, out of great mercy, through the washing of regeneration, You made me a partaker both of the death and of the life of my Savior. Bestow upon me the power of Your Holy Spirit, that I may daily die unto sin, but live unto You and serve You, until in the life to come I shall be wholly renewed and in perfect bliss. Amen. (C. M. Zorn, 1846–1928)

Close by singing or reading in unison "Dearest Jesus, We Are Here," stanzas 1–4 (*LSB* 592; *ELH* 244; *CW* 295; *LW* 226; *LBW* 187; *TLH* 300).

Dearest Jesus, we are here,
    Gladly Your command obeying;
With this child we now draw near
    In response to Your own saying
That to You it shall be given
As a child and heir of heaven.

Your command is clear and plain,
    And we would obey it duly:
"You must all be born again,
    Heart and life renewing truly,
Born of water and the Spirit,
And My kingdom thus inherit."

Therefore we have come to You,
    In our arms this infant bearing.
Truly here Your grace we view;
    May this child, Your mercy sharing,
In Your arms be shielded ever,
Yours on earth and Yours forever.

Gracious Head, Your member own;
  Shepherd, take Your lamb and feed it;
Prince of Peace, make here Your throne;
  Way of Life, to heaven lead it;
Precious Vine, let nothing sever
From Your side this branch forever.

✂ Session 3 ✂

Fruit Basket

Our Goals for This Session

By the power of the Spirit working through God's Word, we want

- the Spirit to produce the fruit of the Spirit in our lives.

Where Are We Going?

How is your war going? Oh yes, you are at war! Living the baptismal lifestyle is a life of warfare between the Spirit and the flesh.

People are born sinful. You don't have to teach children to sin—it comes naturally! Jesus said it clearly in John 3 to Nicodemus. Look at that section again. Remember this: that which is born of flesh is flesh; that which is born of Spirit is spirit (see John 3:6). In Baptism you are perfectly forgiven. But you are not perfect! Christians sin daily, in thought, in words, and in what they do. Sins are what Christians do. Sin is the condition from which Christians suffer. Forgiveness for the condition, as well as for actual sins, was gained at the cross where Jesus paid the price once and for all. But the war goes on as the Holy Spirit works to transform the Christian through Word and Sacrament.

34. How is that warfare evident in your life? Think about how you are conscious of the struggle between the "flesh and the Spirit" in your own life. Describe that struggle to someone else. Listen to his or her struggle.

35. Someone has said, "Satan is not so much interested in getting Christians to do wrong as he is in getting them to think or believe something wrong." Do you agree? Why or why not? How is the statement true or false in your war?

36. What is your major weapon in the war against the flesh? What do you fall back on for help? Prayer? The Word? Other Christians? Talk about it.

Into the Word

Welcome to the War!

37. Read Ephesians 6:10–18. Describe the "war" as Paul sees it (see especially v. 12). What does his description mean to you?

a. What does the apostle Paul suggest you put on? What is the purpose of such "armor"? How would that armor be evident in your life?

b. Describe the pieces of armor suggested (vv. 14–17). What does each mean to you? What is the value of each?

c. What is the "ultimate" weapon according to verse 17?

d. What is the role of prayer in the war? How does that weapon work for you?

38. Going into battle with rulers and authorities can be scary. But it's part of the baptismal life. The power you have is greater than the power of Satan. As a baptized child of God, you are of God because God's Spirit is in you.

a. Study 1 John 4:1–4. State the comfort and assurance you have in your own words (look especially at v. 4). Share that assurance with someone else.

b. Now look at Romans 8:31–39. Living the baptismal lifestyle is living in the almighty power of God. How can a Christian live a really victorious life? What would be the evidence of such a life?

c. As a sinful human being, you can and will stumble. But God can use stumbling humans in powerful ways! Remember David—he sinned by taking Bathsheba. Abraham lied about Sarah to save his life. Elijah wandered out in the wilderness and asked to die. Peter denied Jesus. What others can you name? Recall how each of these failing people was forgiven and used by God for His purpose again. (Check a Bible dictionary if you have forgotten the details of the accounts.) Discuss what the experiences of these biblical people say to you. What comfort can you find? How does God reveal His forgiveness in these cases?

The Vine and Branches

In John 15:1–27, Jesus pictures Himself as the Vine. We are the branches, and the good we are able to do by the Spirit's power is the fruit we produce. Baptism brings us into relationship with Jesus, through forgiveness of sins. The Holy Spirit comes to live in us, and we are empowered to produce fruit—acts of Christian living.

39. What are some of these acts that spring from your Baptism? List them as a group, and discuss some of them. Is the list the same for everyone? Why or why not?

40. Look at John 15:12. What is the command? When has that command to love been difficult for you? If you are willing, share one of those times.

41. When has God prompted you to do something that is difficult for you? When has it been difficult for you to witness to Jesus or to serve or forgive another? Share your experiences

and feelings with the group. How is the struggle evidence that the war still goes on?

42. Another fruit of the Spirit in us is prayer. Look at Romans 8:26–27. What does the text say about the concerns we sometimes have that our prayers sound proper and acceptable? In what sense are our prayers to be childlike?

43. Look at Matthew 7:18–20; 12:33–35; and Luke 6:43–45. Discuss the word of warning you find. How does that warning make us depend even more fully on the forgiveness of Jesus and His power in us?

Fruit of the Spirit

The Spirit comes to us in Baptism. He acts through us to produce His works among His people. Read Galatians 5:16–26.

44. What instruction concerning our life in the Spirit do you find in verses 16–18, 24–25? How is life in the Spirit described? How is it contrasted to life in the flesh?

45. Now name the works of the flesh that are listed in verses 19–21a, 26.

46. What warning in verse 21 makes the list of fleshly works very serious? How would you put that warning into your own words?

47. What are the fruit of the Spirit listed in verses 22–23? What does each mean to you? How do you know it when you see it in a fellow Christian?

48. How are you doing in demonstrating the fruit of the Spirit? Do others see those fruit in you? Share some of your insights with others. Why is such a look at self always the occasion for repentance? How can we find encouragement and renewal in the forgiveness we have in Jesus?

Conclusion

What strategies can you and your class generate that would help to promote fruitful living among the people in your church? List some of them. Discuss them. How can you put some into action?

In Closing

Ask volunteers to include some of the following in short closing prayers:

- Thank God for your Baptism.
- Thank God for the gift of the Holy Spirit that you received at the time of your Baptism.
- Ask God, in a spirit of repentance, to forgive all the works of the flesh.
- Ask God to give you the strength and power to put down the flesh so that the Spirit can produce an abundance of fruit in your life.

One of the dangers, of course, in discussing the fruit of the faith is that we might get the idea that we are saved by what we do. Salvation is through Christ alone. God's grace offers His free gift of salvation through Jesus' death on the cross and His resurrection. But Scripture is also clear that faith without the action is not faith. A good tree will bear fruit.

Look for some of the evidences of fruit in the lives of others. List some of them. Bring your list to class and be ready to share the fruit you discovered as they lived out their baptismal relationship with our Savior.

Prayer: Help me, O God, help me that in true faith I may securely hold the great and saving treasures which You have given me through Baptism! Help me to do this through Your Holy Spirit, whom You have poured out abundantly in Baptism. Help me to nevermore lose the forgiveness of sins and life eternal which You have given me! Amen. (C. M. Zorn, 1846–1928)

Close by singing or reading in unison "All Who Believe and Are Baptized" (*LSB* 601; *CW* 299; *LW* 225; *LBW* 194; *TLH* 301).

All who believe and are baptized
　　Shall see the Lord's salvation;
Baptized into the death of Christ,
　　They are a new creation.
Through Christ's redemption they shall stand
Among the glorious, heav'nly band
　　Of ev'ry tribe and nation.

With one accord, O God, we pray:
　　Grant us Your Holy Spirit.
Help us in our infirmity
　　Through Jesus' blood and merit.
Grant us to grow in grace each day
That by this sacrament we may
　　Eternal life inherit.

∞ Session 4 ∞

Family Reunion

Our Goals for This Session

By the power of the Spirit working through God's Word, we want to

- know and celebrate the privileges and challenges of being part of a Christian community.

Where Are We Going?

In Baptism, the "I" becomes "we." We are baptized into a group, a Christian community, called a congregation. When we were born physically, God saw fit to put us into families. That's His plan. It's the way He sees that we don't starve. In the family, we are nurtured, cared for, and guided to maturity.

When we were reborn in Baptism, we entered another family, the Church. It's called a lot of things in the Bible: the Body of Christ, branches, sheep, the temple of living stones, the priesthood of all believers, and the Bride of Christ.

49. Many people today think of the Church primarily as an organization or a building. Consequently, they talk about the Church as something you go to or something that you join—after you shop around. Read over the biblical images of the Church listed above. What does each say about the

Church? What characteristic does each emphasize? Which, do you think, is most important? Why?

Into the Word

Becoming His Family

50. Read Titus 3:3–11. This is a "before and after" testimony centering on the miracle of Baptism.

    a. What are people like before they are God's people (see especially v. 3)? What evidence for such a description do you see in people around you?

    b. Who initiates the action? Why can Baptism rightly be called an act of God (see vv. 4–7)?

    c. Notice that in verse 7 the idea of "heirs" or "inheritors" is used. When people are baptized, they become heirs of God's promises, His riches. They are family. In verse 8, what does the Bible say family members should do? What should family members avoid (v. 9)? How do you see those characteristics in the members of your family? in you?

Now a Child

51. In Baptism, people become the children of God. As God's children, they receive the Holy Spirit and become heirs to what God has promised in Jesus Christ. See Galatians 4:1–7. What are the main differences between being a slave and being a child? How does that difference affect you?

52. In the previous section (Galatians 3:26–29) the connection is made between Baptism and being children of God. What does that connection mean for your life? How is that connection evident in you?

A Special Saving

53. In 1 Peter 3:18–22, the Church is compared to Noah's ark, and the flood is compared to Baptism. What saving took place in the ark? How is that saving similar to what happens in Baptism?

54. Read 1 Peter 3:18–22. Notice the connection in verse 21 between Baptism and the resurrection of Jesus Christ. Look at verse 22 and see the promise of power through Jesus Christ. What does that power mean for you? for your congregation?

Talk about it. What evidence of that power do you see? How might that power be more evident?

His Bride/Body

Read Ephesians 5:25–30.

55. Here the Church is called the Bride of Christ. What does that image mean for the Church? How is that an important concept in understanding the love of Jesus for His people?

56. Baptism here is called the "washing of water with the Word." See especially verse 32. What does that washing have to do with the Bride/Bridegroom relationship? What does it mean to you?

57. This section also calls the Church the Body of Christ. What does it mean to you to say that you are part of the Body of Christ? What should it mean to your congregation? How will both you and the congregation show that you are part of His Body?

58. What plan can you come up with that will help people in your congregation understand what it means to be loved by Christ as His Bride and to be related so closely to Him that we

are a part of His Body? How might your congregation be stronger if those truths were clearer?

The Body at Work

Ephesians 4:1–6 shows us how this family or Body really works. Notice how this text relates to the custom of having sponsors at a Baptism. Sponsors simply reflect, in an intensified and direct way, the care and concern of the entire Body.

59. Perhaps you are a sponsor. As a group, list some of the duties of a sponsor. How important are these duties? How are they representative of the whole congregation?

60. In the Baptism ceremony, the sponsor is asked to pray for and encourage the child. Look over your list of duties. Now make a list of qualifications for a sponsor. What kind of people should be chosen as sponsors? What part would their faith, their love for the Lord, their part in the Body play in those qualifications? Talk about it. Why should sponsors be chosen carefully?

Unity in Diversity

61. In Ephesians 4:7, a strange paradox is revealed. The unity of the Body of Christ is reflected in the diversity of gifts

given to Christians by the Spirit. Using the unique gifts the Spirit has given you is one of the key ways in which you live your Baptism in daily life. Talk about it. How is the Holy Spirit involved in your life through the gifts and talents He has given you?

62. Read 1 Peter 4:10. What instruction for the use of our gifts do you find there? What does that instruction mean for you as you go about serving others in the Body?

Spiritual Gifts

63. Read about spiritual gifts in Romans 12; 1 Corinthians 12; Ephesians 4; and 1 Peter 4:10. What do the texts say to you about your spiritual gifts? How does the Spirit make it possible for you to serve?

64. Just as our bodies have different parts, God has given different members of Christ's Body different gifts. He wants every part of the Body to function for the sake of the rest. That kind of service is what it means to live our Baptism. Through Baptism, the Spirit gives gifts so that the Body of Christ can function in the world today. What plan can you come up with to allow each person in your congregation to use his or her gifts more effectively? How can more of them be included in service to others and in ministry to the Body?

Priesthood for All

65. Another way the New Testament talks about everyone being involved in the ministry is the "priesthood of all believers." Read 1 Peter 2:2–10 and Revelation 5:9–10. Summarize the passages. What do they mean to you?

66. While the Office of the Ministry (pastoral office) is certainly important in the Church, the New Testament also emphasizes everyone's call to serve others. The New Testament sees each Christian as a servant. What does it mean to you to know that you are a servant in the Body—one who reaches out with the Good News to others and offers the love and grace of God in what you do and say?

a. What does that truth say about the service of each person in the Body?

b. Why is each important? How can each be made to feel important?

Conclusion

67. Look at Ephesians 4:14–16. This is the result of living your Baptism, functioning as a part of the Body of Christ. In verse 14, what is the danger of remaining spiritual babies and refusing to move forward in discipleship?

a. What is the challenge (v. 15)?

b. What is the result (v. 16)?

c. Why does the Church exist? For what purposes are people who are baptized brought together? Make a list of the things the people of God are called upon, challenged, and empowered to do.

68. Living our Baptism implies loving others, caring for them, witnessing, praying, and serving through spiritual gifts. By focusing on our Baptism as a lifestyle—along with millions of other Christians—we can turn the world upside down for Jesus Christ. List ways in which you can multiply this attitude of living service in your congregation. How can you make your plans happen? Who will help?

In Closing

Ask volunteers to offer short prayers that include some of the following:
- Thank God for the privilege of Bible study.
- Thank God that you are baptized.
- Ask God to live in and through your Baptism.
- Ask God to help you use your spiritual gifts.
- Ask God to help your congregation be effective in making disciples for Jesus Christ.

Prayer: O Lord, gracious Trinity, in my Baptism You regenerated me to be Your child. I now repeat my vow that I will renounce the devil and all his works and all his pomp, and will remain true to You unto death. To this end grant me the power of Your Holy Spirit, O Father, for the sake of Jesus Christ, my Savior, and finally give me the crown of life which You have graciously promised me. Amen. (C. M. Zorn, 1846–1928)

Close by singing or reading in unison "Take My Life and Let It Be," stanzas 1–4 (*LSB* 783; *ELH* 444; *CW* 469; *LW* 404; *LBW* 406; *TLH* 400).

Take my life and let it be
Consecrated, Lord, to Thee;
Take my moments and my days,
Let them flow in ceaseless praise.

Take my hands and let them move
At the impulse of Thy love;
Take my feet and let them be
Swift and beautiful for Thee.

Take my voice and let me sing
Always, only for my King;
Take my lips and let them be
Filled with messages from Thee.

Take my silver and my gold,
Not a mite would I withhold;
Take my intellect and use
Ev'ry pow'r as Thou shalt choose.